LET'S see

Presidents' Day

by Natalie M. Rosinsky

Content Adviser: Julie Richter, Ph.D.,
Independent Scholar and Consultant,
Colonial Williamsburg Foundation

Reading Adviser: Rosemary G. Palmer, Ph.D.,
Department of Literacy, College of Education,
Boise State University

Let's See Library
Compass Point Books
Minneapolis, Minnesota

Compass Point Books
3109 West 50th Street, #115
Minneapolis, MN 55410

Visit Compass Point Books on the Internet at *www.compasspointbooks.com*
or e-mail your request to *custserv@compasspointbooks.com*

On the cover: George Washington holds the Constitution and Abraham Lincoln holds the Emancipation Proclamation in this 1865 lithograph.

Photographs ©: Library of Congress, cover; EyeWire, 4, 10; Corbis, 6; Bettmann/Corbis, 8, 16; Kean Collection/Getty Images, 12; Photodisc, 14, 20; Joyce Naltchayan/AFP/Getty Images, 18.

Creative Director: Terri Foley
Managing Editor: Catherine Neitge
Photo Researcher: Marcie C. Spence
Designers: Melissa Kes and Les Tranby
Educational Consultant: Diane Smolinski

Library of Congress Cataloging-in-Publication Data
Rosinsky, Natalie M. (Natalie Myra)
   Presidents' Day / Natalie M. Rosinsky.
      p. cm. (Let's see)
   Includes bibliographical references (p.) and index.
ISBN 0-7565-0773-1
1. Presidents' Day—Juvenile literature. 2. Washington, George, 1732-1799—Juvenile literature.
3. Lincoln, Abraham, 1809-1865—Juvenile literature. 4. Presidents—United States—Juvenile literature.
I. Title. II. Series.
E176.8.R67 2004
394.261—dc22   2004005018

Table of Contents

*NOTE: In this book, words that are defined in the glossary
are in* **bold** *the first time they appear in the text.*

What Is Presidents' Day?

Presidents' Day is a time to feel pride and respect. On this day, people in the United States remember the country's history. All of the presidents of the United States are honored on this holiday.

It all began, however, with two famous presidents: George Washington and Abraham Lincoln. They accomplished much for their country.

Each year, this **patriotic** holiday takes place on the third Monday in February. Presidents' Day is **celebrated** throughout the United States. Schools, businesses, and government offices are closed for the day.

◀ *The White House in Washington, D.C., is home to the president and his family.*

How Did Presidents' Day Begin?

In 1968, Congress passed a law that told people when to celebrate certain holidays. Presidents' Day was one of them.

The day we celebrate Presidents' Day may be new, but the holiday has roots as old as the country itself. It began as two different holidays. One marked the birth of George Washington. The other celebrated the birthday of Abraham Lincoln.

At the **federal** level, the holiday is still called Washington's Birthday. Congress combined the holidays in 1968 but never officially changed the name. The states, local governments, and some federal agencies use the term Presidents' Day, though.

◄ *Washington was born on February 22, 1732. Lincoln was born on February 12, 1809.*

Why Do We Honor George Washington?

George Washington was a brave general. From 1775 to 1783, he led an army of Americans in the Revolutionary War. They fought to be an independent country. They did not want to be ruled by England.

When the Americans won their **revolution,** Washington was a hero. Some people asked him to be king! He refused. He believed in **democracy** and helped set up the new country's government.

Washington was elected the first U.S. president. He was then reelected to another four-year term.

◄ In a famous battle, George Washington crossed the Delaware River. He surprised and defeated the British in a Revolutionary War battle.

How Have We Honored Washington?

The first public celebration of George Washington's birthday was in 1778. The soldiers under his command at **Valley Forge** played drums and **fifes** in his honor. After he died, more people wanted to honor him.

By 1832, most states held celebrations on February 22, Washington's birthday. Communities had gatherings on that day. Cannons blasted to announce events. People gave speeches and recited poems. These speeches and poems described Washington's mighty deeds and fine character.

Washington's birthplace in eastern Virginia and his home in northern Virginia, named Mount Vernon, became interesting historic places to visit.

◄ *The Washington Monument in Washington, D.C., was built to honor the first president.*

Why Do We Honor Abraham Lincoln?

As a child, Abraham Lincoln was poor. He worked hard to become a lawyer. Lincoln believed slavery was wrong. In public, he often **debated** this subject.

In 1860, Abraham Lincoln became the 16th president of the United States. He led the country during the **Civil War.** The Southern states fought to form a separate country. Lincoln struggled to keep the United States together. In 1863, Lincoln outlawed slavery in the **rebellious** South.

Abraham Lincoln was successful, yet he died for his beliefs. In 1865, President Lincoln was **assassinated.**

◄ *Abraham Lincoln debated the subject of slavery when he ran for president.*

How Have We Honored Lincoln?

Abraham Lincoln's birthday was first celebrated a year after his death. On February 12, 1866, government leaders spoke about Lincoln in the nation's capital. In 1892, Illinois became the first state to make Lincoln's birthday a holiday.

Illinois remains proud that "Honest Abe" lived there for many years. Thirty other states also came to celebrate this holiday.

Lincoln's birthplace in Kentucky, and his home and grave in Illinois, became interesting historic places to visit. The nation also built a monument to Lincoln in Washington, D.C. It is called the Lincoln Memorial.

◄ *The Lincoln Memorial was completed in 1922. It took eight years to build.*

What Are Some Symbols of Presidents' Day?

A writer made up a story about George Washington's youth. He said that Washington was always too noble to fib. Supposedly, young George admitted he had cut down a cherry tree. This **legend** about Washington grew. Cherry trees and small axes called hatchets became **symbols** of this president. They are often seen on Presidents' Day.

The log cabin of Abraham Lincoln's youth is another symbol. He worked hard on the farm and often is pictured reading by firelight. The type of hat, called a stovepipe hat, worn by Lincoln is also a symbol of the holiday.

◀ *In a popular but untrue story, young George Washington cannot tell a lie to his father about chopping down a cherry tree.*

How Do We Observe Presidents' Day Today?

In schools, students read about George Washington and Abraham Lincoln to celebrate Presidents' Day. They write stories and poems about them. Sometimes, students even act in plays about them. Classrooms are decorated with pictures of cherry trees, hatchets, log cabins, stovepipe hats, and the presidents.

Bands play near the monuments to the two presidents. Another **custom** is placing flowers on these monuments. People give speeches. They may learn and give famous speeches that Washington and Lincoln once made. Sometimes, people dress up and act out events from the lives of the two presidents.

◄ *Flower wreaths are placed at the Lincoln Memorial on Presidents' Day.*

How Has Presidents' Day Changed?

In 1971, President Richard Nixon announced that Presidents' Day would honor all U.S. presidents. Since then, people sometimes include other presidents in this celebration. Thomas Jefferson and Franklin D. Roosevelt are often remembered. They, along with others, were also important leaders.

Presidents' Day is the perfect time to think about the men and women who have led the country since its beginning more than 200 years ago. It is a time to think about what qualities make a good president.

It is also fun to think about who will be president when the students of today are grown-ups. Could it be someone you know? Could it be you?

◀ *Mount Rushmore in South Dakota honors four presidents: (from left) George Washington, Thomas Jefferson, Theodore Roosevelt, and Abraham Lincoln.*

Glossary

assassinate—to murder an important person, often for political reasons

celebrate—to enjoy and honor something

Civil War—the war between the Northern and Southern states from 1861 to 1865. The North wanted to keep the states together and ban slavery. The South wanted to be separate and keep slavery. The North won.

custom—something regularly done by a group of people

debated—argued at a planned, public meeting that interested people attend

democracy—a form of government in which the people elect their leaders

federal—having to do with the central government of the United States

fifes—musical instruments that are like small flutes

legend—a tall tale told about a real person

patriotic—helping and loving one's country

rebellious—to fight against authority

revolution—a war fought to change a government

symbols—things that represent something else

Valley Forge—the place in Pennsylvania where Washington's Continental Army spent the cold winter of 1777–1778

Did You Know?

* The capital of the United States, Washington, D.C., is named after George Washington. The state of Washington also has his name.

* President Lincoln grew his beard because a young girl thought he should. Eleven-year-old Grace Bedell wrote to Lincoln about this. She thought he would look much better with whiskers.

* Pictures of Washington and Lincoln appear on United States money and stamps.

* Because different calendars were used when he was born, Washington's birthday is sometimes listed as February 11, 1732.

* The state of Illinois calls itself the Land of Lincoln.

* President Lincoln outlawed slavery in the Southern states that were in rebellion against the Union. Slaves in the North became free when the country added a new law in 1865. It was the 13th Amendment to the U.S. Constitution.

Want to Know More?

At the Library

Cohn, Amy L., and Suzy Schmidt. *Abraham Lincoln.* New York: Scholastic, 2002.

Nettleton, Pamela Hill. *George Washington: Farmer, Soldier, President.* Minneapolis: Picture Window Books, 2004.

Roop, Connie, and Peter Roop. *Let's Celebrate Presidents' Day.* Brookfield, Conn.: The Millbrook Press, 2001.

On the Web

For more information on *Presidents' Day,* use FactHound to track down Web sites related to this book.

1. Go to *www.facthound.com*
2. Type in a search word related to this book or this book ID: 0756507731.
3. Click on the *Fetch It* button.

Your trusty FactHound will fetch the best Web sites for you!

On the Road

George Washington Birthplace National Monument
1732 Popes Creek Road
Washington's Birthplace, VA 22443
804/224-1732
To visit Washington's birthplace near Fredericksburg, Virginia

Mount Vernon
George Washington Memorial Parkway
Mount Vernon, VA 22121
703/780-2000
To visit Washington's historic mansion

Abraham Lincoln Birthplace National Historic Site
2995 Lincoln Farm Road
Hodgenville, KY 42748
270/358-3137
To visit an early 19th-century cabin that represents the one in which Lincoln was born

Lincoln Home National Historic Site
413 S. Eighth St.
Springfield, IL 62701
217/492-4241
To visit Lincoln's home of more than 20 years

Index

About the Author

Natalie M. Rosinsky writes about history, social studies, economics, science, and other fun things. One of her two cats usually sits on her computer as she works in Mankato, Minnesota. Natalie earned graduate degrees from the University of Wisconsin and has been a high school and college teacher.